Forex
For Beginners:
Strategies for Beginners and Experts: 2 in 1 Bundle

Book 1:

Forex for Beginners

The Forex Guide for Making Money with Currency Trading

Contents

Introduction _____ *6*
Chapter 1: Understanding Forex _____ *9*
Chapter 2: Types of Orders _____ *19*
Chapter 3: The Importance of Analysis _____ *23*
Chapter 4: Trading Strategies for Beginners __ *31*
Chapter 5: Risk Management _____ *39*
Chapter 6: Trading Psychology _____ *44*
Chapter 7: Do's and Don'ts to Forex Trading _ *53*
Chapter 8: Tips and Secrets to Success _____ *57*
Chapter 9: Getting Started _____ *64*
Conclusion _____ *68*
Preview of Day Trading for Beginners By Baron McBane _____ *Fel! Bokmärket är inte definierat.*

© **Copyright 2015**

All rights Reserved. No part of this book may be reproduced in any form without permission in writing from the author. Reviewers may quote brief passages in reviews.

Disclaimer

No part of this publication may be reproduced or transmitted in any form or by any means, mechanical or electronic, including photocopying or recording, or by any information storage and retrieval system, or transmitted by email without permission in writing from the publisher.

While all attempts have been made to verify the information provided in this publication, neither the author nor the publisher assumes any responsibility for errors, omissions or contrary interpretations of the subject matter herein.

This book is for entertainment purposes only. The views expressed are those of the author alone, and should not be taken as expert instruction or commands. The reader is responsible for his or her own actions.

Adherence to all applicable laws and regulations, including international, federal, state and local laws governing professional licensing, business practices, advertising and all other aspects of doing business in the US, Canada, UK or any other jurisdiction is the sole responsibility of the purchaser or reader.

Neither the author nor the publisher assumes any responsibility or liability whatsoever on the behalf of the purchaser or reader of these materials. Any perceived slight of any individual or organization is purely unintentional.

Introduction

I want to thank you and commend you for downloading the book, "Forex for Beginners: The Forex Guide for Making Money with Currency Trading".

Within the investment world today are many options where people can or should invest their hard-earned money. Most of these investment options do their best to guarantee growth and profitability. From binary to forex to shares to property to retirement annuities, the list is endless.

You can invest in low-risk investments with a lower profit margin, or you could take a higher risk and gain higher profitability. The options available to you today help you to tailor make your investment portfolio to your character, situations, and financial goals.

One of the popular investment options in the financial world today is forex. Forex took off in the late 1990s with the introduction of the worldwide web. The market became accessible internationally. People far and wide have come to participate in the forex market. Some become successful while others make a string of losses, run out of capital, or become disheartened and give up.

Despite all of this, the forex trading industry continues to see new traders joining their platforms, forums, and world regularly.

So what makes forex worthwhile?

Is it possible to be successful in forex trading?

Those are excellent questions. Ones that I hope to answer and more throughout this book.

In this book, you will find everything you need to know to begin as a new forex trader. I have skipped the financial jargon where possible to give you a guide to forex that is easy to understand, practical and full of examples. However, an understanding of basic forex terminology will go a long way in helping you understand the forex articles you have read and are going to read. After all, forex is a world unto itself, bringing with it its own language.

At the end of this book, you should feel well-informed and prepared to tackle the forex markets. Whether you end up trading forex as a hobby, part-time job, or a career, will be up to you. My goal is to give you the information you need to get started.

From the get go, I want to encourage you to view forex trading as a business. This will go a long way to setting you up for success. Because forex is about educated speculation, a lot of strategy and research goes into forex trading.

In the world of investments and finances, forex is fine art. Attention is paid to detail. Time is spent fine tuning strategies. In this book, you are going to learn what you need to understand and practice financial fine art.

Please be aware that all examples in this book are fictional. They are **not** based on the current forex market and exchange rates. I have used such examples merely to illustrate the concepts of the forex methods listed throughout this book. My goal is to use simple examples to help you understand the concepts well.

Thanks again for downloading this book, I hope you enjoy it!

Chapter 1: Understanding Forex

Within the investment world lies the forex market. Many investors worldwide, whether big or small, come to this large market in the hopes of gaining riches, success, and adrenaline. Nothing compares to the thrill of making a successful trade or the quick reaction to a falling market.

Forex trading is an opportunity to learn, think quickly, strategize and grow. Forex is more than science. Forex is an art.

Can anyone learn forex? Yes! However, forex is complex and intricate. For a person to be successful in forex trading, time, research and dedication are imperative. Let's look more closely at understanding the basics surrounding forex.

What is forex?

Foreign exchange better known as **forex** involves foreign currencies such as the US dollar (USD), the Euro (EUR), British pound (GBP), Japanese Yen (JYP), Australian Dollar (AUD), Swiss Franc (CHF), and so on. Whether you are exchanging different currencies or purchasing stock, the world runs on forex.

When it comes to investments, forex trading is one of the most lucrative investments in the financial world. Banks, businesses, governments, investors, traders and speculators (like you or me) have all at some point in time dealt with forex.

In forex trading, you would trade among the major currencies listed above on the Forex market also known as the "*Fx market*", "*currency market*", "*Foreign exchange currency market*". At the end of the day, it's the same market. This market sees an average turnover of $3 trillion per day.

The Forex market is open 24 hours a day, 5 days a week with its centers located in London, New York, Paris, Sydney, Hong Kong, Singapore, Tokyo, Zurich, and Frankfurt. This is done to strategically keep the market open throughout the week. When the sun sets in New York, business is kept open in the early morning hours of Hong Kong, Singapore, or Tokyo.

The result is a central marketplace where everyone is on the same page. Whether you are a first-time investor or a trader for a large corporation, you all receive the same information regarding the market, dips in currencies, national news, etc., simultaneously. This keeps the playing field fair.

The beauty of the forex market is found in its liquidity. Meaning, when you buy and sell currencies you are never stuck with a product or stock. As a trader, you can sell your currencies at any point in time with the reassurance that someone will buy it. Traders or brokers are always available to buy or sell; thus, you can buy or sell currency any time you choose.

In addition to all of this, the forex market is only impacted by national events such as interest rate hikes or dips, political events and scandals, or changes in national unemployment rates. As a result, no one corporation, bank, or country can adjust the forex market to suit their means or agendas.

On the forex market, anyone can go from an average income to riches. From an investment point of view, the reality of forex trading is that it has high risks for high rewards. The question to ask yourself is: how much risk are you willing to take?

Understanding basic terminology

Whether you are starting out in forex trading or have a background in forex, understanding the terminology associated with forex trading is vital. You are in a new world with its own rules, culture, language, and permutations. Fortunately, forex terminology is relatively easy to understand. Here is some basic jargon with their explanations to help you better understand what people are talking about when they talk forex:

Pip

Pips are also known as a percentage in point. It is a unit of measurement for the movement in price of a currency. In Forex, the pip is the fourth number after the decimal. For example, USD might be at 1.520**0** at the start of the day and ends at 1.522**2**. This means that the USD improved by 2 pips.

Currency pairs

Whenever you buy currency it comes in pairs. For example, USDJPY which is the *Dollar Yen"* or GBP/USD which is known as *"Sterling"*. Currency pairs consist of two components: the base currency and the quote currency.

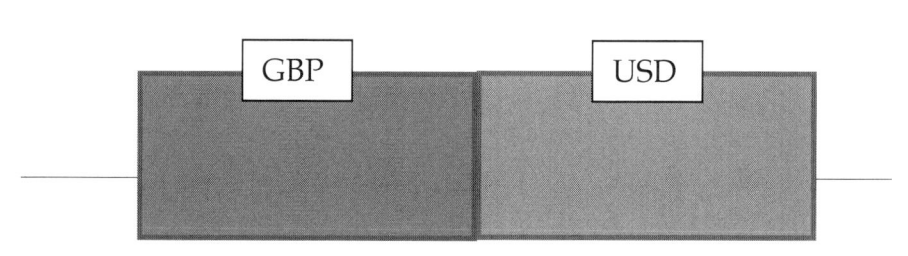

| GBP | USD |

| Base Currency – valued at 1 | Quote Currency – the amount needed to get one British Pound |

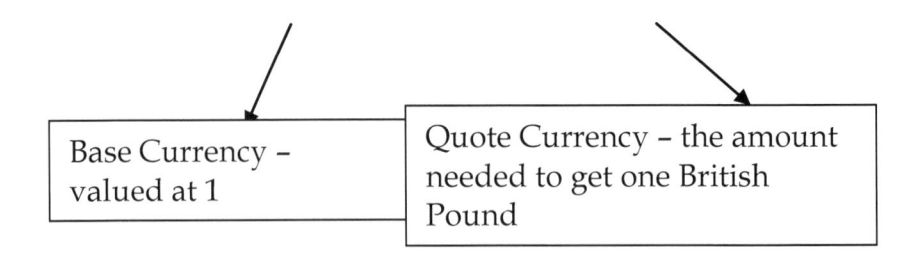

For example, you want to buy GBP with your dollars. The exchange rate is 1.2500 USD for 1 GBP. The GBP is your base currency and USD is your quote currency. The quote currency will fluctuate during the day or the week's trading. Today it may be 1.2500 USD to 1 GBP but by Friday the exchange rate may be 1.2750 USD to 1 GBP. The base currency is constant while the quote currency fluctuates.

This holds true for all currency pairs except the Japanese pairs. The Japanese currency is devalued against the other currencies (we are trading in major currencies.) As a result, the pip becomes the second digit after the decimal. For example, the exchange rate of the USD/JPY may be 88.1500 thus the pip is the number 5.

To help you identify currency pairs, see the below table for easy reference

Major Forex Pairs	Nicknames
EUR/USD	Euro
USD/JPY	Dollar Yen
GBP/USD	Sterling or Cable
USD/CHF	Swissy
USD/CAD	Dollar Canada or Loonie
AUD/USD	Aussie Dollar

NZD/USD	Kiwi

Spread
The spread is the amount that your chosen broker is willing to pay for your currency and sell you currency. Look at it as a commission fee.

For example, you want to buy GBP/USD at an exchange rate of 1.1552. Your broker will sell you GBP at a rate of 1.1555 USD. Thus you will buy your British pounds at a higher price. When you want to sell your GBP/USD, your broker will purchase your currency at a rate of 1.1550, two pips less.

This is how your broker makes money. This is spread. When it comes to choosing a broker, you want to find a broker with the lowest spread while giving you great benefits. This is why researching your broker is vital.

Bids
When you are looking to sell currency, the bid is the highest price that you can get your broker to pay you for your currency.

Ask
When you are wanting to buy currency, the ask is the lowest price that your broker will sell the currency to you.

Trading platform
Trading platform is where you will request to buy or sell your currency pairs. This is the forum where you communicate with your broker. Here you will tell your broker when you want to sell, the quantity you are looking for, when you will take your profit or your loss, and so on.

The broker that you choose should have its own platform that you can use for your forex trading.

Positions, entries, and exits
When you buy your currency pair you have opened your position on the forex market. This is also called an entry.
When you sell your currency pair you have closed your position and exit the market. This is when you exit.

Leverage
Let's assume that you have found yourself a great broker. You are now wanting to trade. First you need to deposit some money into your margin account (the account that you have with your broker). Let's say you deposit $1,000. Your broker will then allow you to trade $100,000 dollars. The leverage on this trade will be 100:1. The standard leverage ratios are 50:1, 100:1 or 200:1 depending on the broker you choose. Sometimes the ratios can go as high as 400:1. The higher the ratio, the higher your risk of loss or gain depending on the market.

The idea of leverage is to help you trade with large amounts of money while using the bare minimum of your own money.
The risk with leverage is that as much as what you can gain, you can lose. This is why understanding stop and limit orders is going to be important for your trading strategy (see chapter 2).

Margin

In order to have leverage you need to have a margin. Margin is the amount of money you deposit into your account with your broker. This money is then used to open your "*position*". All brokers have a margin percentage that they require. This margin varies and may be 1%, 2%, or 0.5%. It all depends on the broker. Once you know your margin requirements you will be able to calculate your leverage.

Below are a few margin types that you will come across in your trading experience:
- *Account margin* – The total amount of money in your account.
- *Used margin* – The amount of money that is locked or untouchable. This is what the broker will use to keep your current positions open. This money is only available to you when you close your position.
- *Usable margin* – The money available to open new positions.

Long vs Short

Keeping a forex trade open for a week or longer is called a long position. In this type of position, you are riding a long trend.

A short position is when you sell one currency against another because you expect it to depreciate. For example, buying GBP with USD because you expect the USD exchange rate to the GBP to drop. Thus you hope to make more GBP for the same amount of USD you are trading with.

Risk to reward ratio

This ratio shows you the amount of risk you are prepared to take on a single trade and how much profit you will make if the market is in your favor.

For example, you are prepared to lose $50 on a trade and you are hoping to gain $100. The risk to reward ratio is 5:10 since you are risking $50 to gain $100

Rollover
Since the forex market works on currency pairs, rollover pertains to two different interest rates. These interest rates are based on the overnight rates in which banks borrow money from each other.
You get a positive rollover when the currency you bought is higher than the currency you sold. If the opposite happens, you get a negative rollover.
Rollover only occurs to those trades that have an open position at 17:00 sharp. The next morning you will be able to receive the rollover.

Forex markets
The forex market is in itself a market. Within the forex market are three variations, namely the stop market, options market, and the forward market. These variations come into play in the strategy you will use in your forex trading. Therefore, knowing a little bit more about them will go a long way in helping you to determine your trading strategy and the type of broker you look for.
However, due to the complexity of the options market, I am only going to mention the spot market and forward (futures) market.

Spot market

The spot market is where traders can complete their trades immediately. It is also known as the "physical" or "cash" market. Here you can sell and buy immediately with the transaction being completed within two business days. In this type of market, you get to capitalize on the currency exchange rate and other factors immediately before any fluctuations impact on your profits, causing you losses.

Forward market
The forward market, also known as the futures market, can take weeks to months to conclude a trade. The transaction is set with a predetermined currency exchange rate for an agreed upon date.

How does forex work

In a nutshell, forex trading is the speculation that one currency will do better than another. For example, the USD is said to rise against the EUR; as a trader you may decide to buy the EUR/USD in the hopes of buying Euros at a cheaper price and selling them to gain a profit from the strength of the US dollar.
Forex trading involves watching the fx market for trends, highs and lows. You are watching it carefully, strategically, and analytically. From your understanding of the market and the information you gather from experts in the market, you are able to make an educated guess as to what currency you want to buy or sell at a specific point in time. You will carefully calculate the amount of risk that you are willing to take in the event of a loss.
Through it all, the successful trader understands that emotions cannot be involved in this form of trading. For trading to be successful, you have to be prepared to lose in order to gain.

Forex trading is gutsy and definitely not for the faint of heart.

Chapter 2: Types of Orders

Now that we know what the forex market is, how it works, and some basic terminology, let's take a look at the types of orders you may use within your trading.

The type of broker and trading platform you use will determine which orders you will implement in your trading. These order types are available to help you enter and exit your trade while limiting your losses and taking your profits. They are part of the tools you will use to execute your trading.

The below order types include basic and common types of orders.

Market order
The market order is a basic and standard order. This order is responsible for helping you buy or sell currency pairs at the best price available at that specific moment in time. Once you have placed the order, you immediately receive your purchase. This makes the market order a quick, reliable way to get in and out of trades.

Stop-entry order
In trading you can either watch the forex market like a hawk eyeing its prey, waiting for that moment when it can swoop down for the kill. Alternatively, you can use a stop-entry order to do the watching for you while you continue with the rest of your bucket list.

A stop-entry order is used when you want to sell your currency pair as the market drops and buy currency as it rises. The expectation is that the market will continue to follow the same pattern it has already shown.

Limit-entry order

The limit-entry order is the opposite of the stop-entry order since it predicts that the market will behave opposite to what it has been once it hits your specific price. Thus, you will sell currency when the market rises and buy when the market drops.

Stop Loss

This order puts into place a stop on your trade according to a pre-determined amount of time. For example, you buy GBP/USD and put a limit of 50 pips. The currency can only fall to 50 pips below your purchase rate before stopping your trade.

This order helps prevent large losses and keeps emotions in check. It also helps manage the finances in your trading account before they run out. After all, you can only spend what you have.

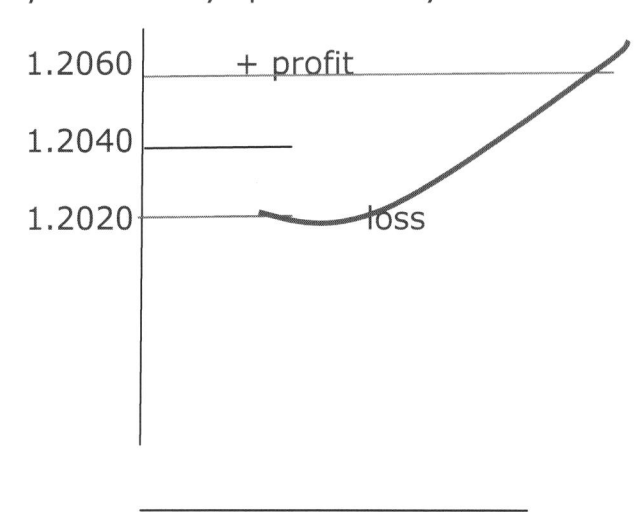

```
1.2060 |_____ + profit _____
1.2040 |_____
1.2020 |_____ loss
```

In the above chart we see that if you buy a currency pair with a stop loss at 1.2040 you will gain profit when the rate reaches 1.2060. but make a loss if it drops to 1.2020. The stop loss order keeps your limit to a loss of 20 pips.

Take profit

The take profit order determines when you will cash in your profits. This order doesn't require you to pay any commission to your broker.

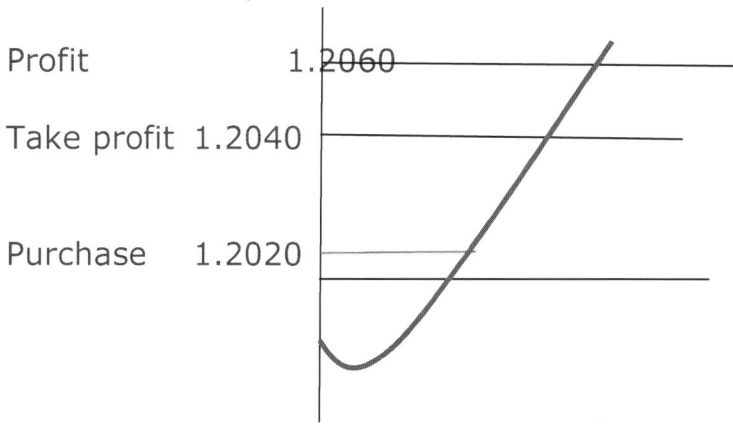

```
Profit              1.2060
Take profit  1.2040
Purchase     1.2020
```

In the above chart, you purchase GBP/USD for 1.2020 and set a take profit order at 1.2040. You make 20 pips profit. The trend continues to climb with your take profit order guaranteeing you a profit of 20 pips.

Trailing stop

In a trailing stop order you will place a stop-loss each time you trade while carefully monitoring your loss and the market trends. You follow the dips in the trends until the market swings and starts to climb. At this point you will move your stop-loss to keep the profit you've already made. If the market is climbing, you make profit while monitoring your stop loss in order to keep your losses at a minimum. The last thing you want is to lose all the profit you would've made.

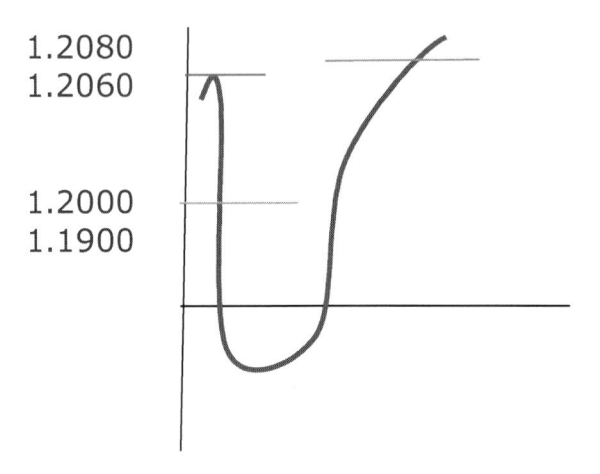

1.2080
1.2060

1.2000
1.1900

In this chart, you buy GBP/USD for 1.2060. The market goes on a steep dip, dropping to 1.1900. Your stop order is set for 1.2000. You continue to follow the market and reset your stop to 1.2060 as it climbs back up. You have now made back the money you lost. However, you continue to follow the market and place another stop order at 1.2080. You have now exercised the trailing stop order and have made a profit of 20 pips.

Chapter 3: The Importance of Analysis

Any forex trader needs to utilize analysis as part of their trading strategy. This helps them to know when to buy or sell, what order they want to place, and when to enter the market.
Forex trading success is linked to information and timing. A trader must know what is going on in the economic and national world since any large scale events could bring either profit or potential loss.

Two main types of analysis are used by forex traders: the fundamental analysis and the technical analysis. In this chapter, I am going to expand on both to give you a clear understanding of how they work and their importance.
Should you have only one type of analysis in your trading strategy? That depends on your style of trading. Both types of analysis are important. Some traders prefer technical while others prefer fundamental. Other traders enjoy using a mix of technical and fundamental analysis. The choice is yours. The key is understanding these types of analysis.

Fundamental Analysis
For those of you who are investors or people interested in the financial market, you may have noticed that every year when your nation's finance minister makes their speech on the nation's financial budget, budget cuts, and approaches to other financial aspects of the country, your local currency either improves or worsens.

This is the time when fundamental investors are sitting on the edge of their seats, their eyes glued to their computer screens as they watch with hawk-like eyes the movement of the global financial markets. Which currencies are going up and which are coming down in response to this speech? They wait. Anticipation fills the air.

These investors have an educated gut instinct that is helping them predict their next move. Still they wait. Poised. Ready. At the appropriate time they will either buy or sell their currencies.

To these investors, fundamental analysis is key. Fundamental analysis hinges on economic and national events or changes that have a direct impact on currency. Fluctuations in interest rates, unemployment, or political news will bring about fluctuations in the forex market. Generally, fundamentalists are able to predict the patterns that will follow such events or changes.

The key with fundamental analysis is to understand the market that you are analyzing. You can't be an expert on multiple markets. For fundamental analysis to be effective, you need to work towards being an expert in one market. This may be the US or Britain or Japan for instance.

However, if you decide to use fundamental analysis with technical analysis, you are able to have a finger in a few pies. You are able to watch the markets you are working with while simultaneously being aware of economic and national events.

Most forex trading platforms provide an economic calendar to help keep track of important government events, interest hikes, supply and demand, changes to unemployment rates, etc.

Technical Analysis
Technical analysis involves looking at past patterns and trends in order to predict future patterns and trends. In some ways it relies on self-fulfilling prophecies. If you look at history regardless of topic, you will find a lot of similar patterns and behaviors have been repeated over the years. Fashion is one such example. People are creatures of habit.

Traders who prefer or use technical analysis as part of their trading strategy rely on these habits and repeated patterns or trends to help them make profit from their investments.

One of the common mistakes beginner or inexperienced traders make is that of starting a trade too early or too late. What do I mean by this?
Let's assume that you are going to buy the USD/GDP currency. You make your purchase of GDP thinking that you are going to make a profit since the GDP has dropped in value and should, in theory, turn and appreciate again. Unfortunately, the GDP continues to drop by another 50 pips. Not wanting to lose more money, you pull out of the trade. The day after you stopped the trade, the GDP turns and for the rest of the week climbs back up passing the rate you bought yesterday. By the end of the week's trade, you would've recovered your losses and come out with a 20 pip profit. Ouch.

Technical analysis helps traders, experienced and non-experienced, to more accurately gauge when to start a trade, when to stop a trade, and how to place their orders to keep their losses to a minimum.

For a person who loves charts and math, technical analysis is right up your alley. Technical analysis uses charts, including price charts and volume charts, indicators, and other mathematical representations to identify the best time to begin or end a trade, the length a trade should be (long or short), and the sustainability of the market toward that trade.

Tips to successful technical analysis

Technical analysis is quite complex. Besides encouraging you to do more research on the topic, I thought I'd include a few quick tips to help you with your technical analysis:

1. **Don't neglect your charts**. Charts are a crucial aspect of your analysis. Be sure to use daily and weekly charts in your analysis. Forex trading follows economic cycles which take years to complete. As a result, your weekly to monthly charts will be able to show you major trends. Your day charts are going to help you pinpoint when you should enter a trade and exit a trade.
2. **Support and resistance**. The goal of a support level is to stop prices from dropping past a certain point. Resistance works similarly to a ceiling; it tries to stop prices from rising above this ceiling. Support and resistance are great indicators of when to open or close your trades. It shows you the supply and demand of the currency pairs you are wanting to trade with.

    Here is an example of support and resistance:

3. **Understand breakout**. In a nutshell breakout occurs when the currency pair price rises above the level of resistance and is sold below the level of support. Usually the price will go higher instead of dropping. When this happens a new "trend" begins.
4. **Use momentum indicators**. Momentum indicators increase the odds of a successful trade. The RSI (Relative Strength Index) is one such indicator referred to by several trading strategies and forex experts.

Price action analysis

Besides fundamental and technical analysis, another analysis comes into play. Price action analysis. This analysis strips your charts of all indicators and allows you to trade on the raw price action.

Price action analysis focuses on helping you find recurring price patterns. These patterns will in turn help you predict future trends in prices. To look for these trends, you will focus on two trends:

Downtrend – Look for patterns of low highs (LH) and low lows (LL).
Uptrend – Patterns of high highs (HH) and high lows (HL)

Price action analysis will help you to know who is losing control of the currency: the buyers or sellers? This will help you find the reversals in the current trends from which you will trade accordingly either selling or buying depending on your trading strategy.
Price action analysis comes into play with swing trading, a topic for another day.

Understanding charts

Charts are a visual presentation of what is happening in prices and the market. They are a necessary part of technical analysis. Let's look at three common charts:

Line chart

The line chart is the simplest chart available to traders. The prices of the currency pair you are trading is shown on the side of the chart while the date is at the bottom. A line is used to mark the closing price of a trade on each day. Thus a line chart is used as a monthly or weekly chart or even longer. A line chart is ideal to pick up on moving averages or momentum.

Bar chart

A bar chart consists of a string of bars. Each bar consists of a vertical line which represents the price action of a day; the highest price is at the top of the line and the lowest price is the bottom of the line. The horizontal lines of the bar indicate the open (left line) and closing (right line) points of a trade. Below is an example of what a bar looks like

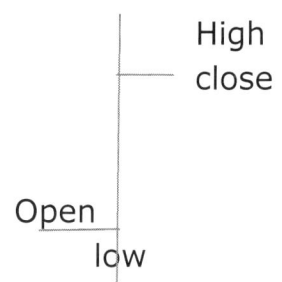

```
          | High
          ├── close
          │
   Open __│
        low
```

A bar chart can be used to analyze daily, weekly, or monthly activity.

Candlestick

The Japanese candlestick is claimed to have been one of the oldest methods of analysis in trade history. The candlestick is similar to the bar chart in the information you receive. A candlestick chart comprises of a series of candlesticks. Each candle represents one unit of time (a day, an hour, etc.). Depending on the platform you use, the colors of the candlesticks will vary. A candlestick is made up of two components:

1. The candle or body showing the price of a unit at its opening and closing. Assuming the candlestick chart is using the colors green and red as per the example below. A candle colored in red shows that the trade was closed at a price

lower than it was opened. If the candle is green, then the opposite applies.
2. The wick or shadow is the two lines at either side of the candle. These shadows illustrate the highs and lows of the price.

Chapter 4: Trading Strategies for Beginners

Do you remember the time when you first learned how to ride a bicycle? Your parents probably bought you a tricycle to teach you how to pedal a bike when you were a toddler. As you got older, you were promoted to a bicycle with training wheels. As you rode, your confidence would rise and unbeknownst to you, your parents took a wrench and secretly raised the training wheels off the ground. You continued to ride blissfully while subconsciously working on your balance.

After some time, the day finally arrived when your training wheels were removed. Now was the time to ride unaided. You started off nervous, wobbly. One of your parents held the handlebars with one hand while the other hand supported your seat. Off you went, shouting *Don't let go!*
You look behind you. Realization hits you. You're doing it! You are riding your bike on your own. You fall! Your parent is by your side immediately helping you dust off and pick the bicycle up. You climb back on. It didn't matter that you fell; what mattered is that you didn't give up.

Trading strategies for beginners are the same as training wheels on a bicycle. They are a tool to get you started. They come with the intention of helping build your confidence while you learn the art of forex trading. The point is to give you an idea that you can expand on. The purpose is for you to come up with your own trading strategy, tailor-made to suit your trading style, needs, and personality.

Forex trading strategies are a dime a dozen. They range from simple to advanced. Although I am going to elaborate on a handful of trading strategies, I encourage you to experiment with them. When you find a trading strategy that seems to be working well for you, see what you can do to enhance and improve it.

Regardless of the strategy you use, you will still need to do your analysis, implement your order types, decide on your risk, and control your emotions. These are the fundamentals of forex trading.

Trend Trading
Within the forex trading world is the expression that *trends are your friends*. Trend trading is a strategy used by many traders both advanced and beginner. The basic goal is to identify the strongest trends in the market. Once you have done this, you can open a trade.

With trend trading, you do not have to worry about finding that perfect entry and exit point in your trade. The important part is that you enter the trade.

Your technical analysis and charts will assist you in identifying which trend is the strongest. As a trader you are looking for those currency pairs that are trading up or down.

Another tool that is helpful in finding trends is the RSI indicator, also known as the Relative Strength Index. Its job is to identify the strength of the currency pairs as well as show you when a price reversal can be expected.

As with any trading strategy, knowing when to exit a trade is helpful. In the trend trading strategy, you will want to place a limit order and stop order. You will base these orders on your risk to reward ratio.
Here are some tips to creating a trend trading strategy:

1. **Research.** Spend some time studying your charts and implementing your analysis. Watching the market closely will help you find the overall trend of the currencies. You will also need to decide when is a good time to enter the trend. Entering a trend toward the end before it turns may not be the best idea unless you enjoy the thrill of risky trading.
2. **Enter the trend**. Once you have identified the trend, open your trading position.
3. **Ride the trend** until you see that it is about to reverse. There is no point in riding a reversal and making large losses.
4. **Exit the trade**. As you see the trend begin to turn or coming close to a reversal trend, you need to sell. Sell your currency pairs and close your trading position.

The point of trend trading is to ride the trend for as long as it is in your favor. When the trend stops being favorable, shake hands and part ways.

Day Trading

Irrespective of experience, day trading is popular among experienced traders and novices. Traders who use day trading will make several trades throughout the course of the day before closing all trades at night.

Day trading is time consuming, since you have to monitor the market and your trades regularly. Day trading aims to have accumulative profit at the end of the day.

The key to day trading is making trades quickly. The longer your trading position stays open the higher you are of encountering a loss. Your goal is to ride the small price fluctuations to find your profits.

Here are a few tips for day trading to help you be successful:

1. **Wait for any market volatility to settle**. This often pertains to news. When news or events are released, don't trade; the market is volatile and unpredictable at this point.
2. **Stick to your risk limit of 1% or less per day of trading**. You want to ensure that what you lose in a day can be made back the next day. The last thing you want is to see a significant decrease in your capital.
3. **Don't open a trade before a news or event is released**. You may know what that news is but you cannot tell how the market will react. Rather, wait to see what happens and trade later.

Scalp trading

Another way of describing scalp trading is micro trading. In scalp trading, a trader looks to make very frequent trades often looking at charts that show the market movements within the past minute. A scalper will also be making trades with a few profitable pips.

For example, you may decide that you are going to scalp trade. You set your analysis to reflect the happenings of the currencies and market for the past couple of minutes. You ensure that you have a high leverage. Each pip is valued at $10. You decide that you are going to work on 6 pips per trade. One successful trade then equals $60. You may complete 10 successful trades in the day thus walking away with a $600 profit.

When scalp trading, you need to include in your calculations the amount of spread you will be paying. This is important. A scalper will pay the broker the relevant spread as they buy currency pairs. To come out profitable, you need to make sure that your profitable trades cover the spread and more otherwise you only break even.

Although scalping is a form of day trading. I recommend leaving this type of trading until you are confident as a trader. Scalping requires intense concentration, confidence, and responsiveness. You open a trade and close it within minutes. Scalping is for certain personalities, and not every trader is suitable for scalp trading.

Fading

The fading day trading strategy requires a forex trader to buy currency on the market dip and sell on the market high. A trader using this strategy is predicting the demise of their currency pair whilst most of the general forex traders will hold their stocks and "go long".

Fading assumes that forex is overbought and tries to capitalize on the emotions of the other traders. A trader may be ready to sell in order to get profits or the market is getting volatile and making some traders nervous.

Fading is a high risk, high reward strategy.

Daily Pivots
With the daily pivot strategy, a trader will take advantage of the market's volatility. You would open your trade by buying at the lowest price of the day while selling when the currency rate is at its highest. This high just before the market reverses again. Similar to range trading with the difference being that you are closing your position each day and not leaving it open for a lengthy period of time.

Range Trading
Range trading takes advantage of the price fluctuations in a day throughout a week or a longer period. It holds the view that each currency remains relatively constant within its fluctuations.

Before using range trading, you'll need to make use of your analysis techniques. You need to be able to identify the currency trends and trading signals. When is the best time to buy currency? When do you sell to close your trade and cash in the profits of your trade?
When the market is lacking a specific trend or direction, range trading can be a useful strategy. Here's how you would go about range trading:

1. **Identify the range**. Range is located between the support and resistance zones. A support zone is the point where you would buy into the market; the resistance zone is when you would sell to close your trade. Basically you are looking for the high and low patterns.
2. **Entry and risk management**. Your broker may provide you with some tools such as oscillators to help you pinpoint your point of entry. In layman's terms, you will look for the lowest drop in the currency rate and buy into the trade. As you are doing that you need to determine your risk to reward ratio. How much are you prepared to risk? A stop loss order will assist you in managing your risk.
3. **Repeat.**

For a novice trader, range trading provides a more consistent profit than some of the other forex trading strategies.

Some traders find one trading strategy that works for them whereas other traders may use multiple strategies to implement according to the movement of the forex market. When planning your trading habits and methodology, consider the pros and cons of having a single trading strategy vs multiple strategies. Along with these pros and cons consider your personality and character.

Whatever decision you make, work towards creating your own tailor made forex experience.

Chapter 5: Risk Management

In chapter one, we spoke about some basic forex terminology, one of them being the risk to reward ratio. I want to expand on this topic. Risk management is all about managing your risk versus reward. This is key to being successful in your trading.

In this chapter, I want to not only explain the importance of risk management, but also give you some practical ways of implementing it into your trading strategy. I want to help you know how to manage your losses so that you still make a profit or keep your losses to a minimum thereby helping you trade another day.

Risk management is what makes forex trading a business and not a gambling expedition. If a trader does not manage their risk and approaches forex with the mindset of *I'm going to make a huge profit,* then they are gambling. Forex trading is all about educated speculation and risk management.

All about risk
You can lose on any trade. No trade is exempt from loss. Thus, you need to calculate the amount of risk you are prepared to take on every trade you do. On average you would risk 1% or 2% of your account.

For example, you have an account of $10,000 and you want to risk one percent of this account on your trade. $10,000*1% = $100. This means that you are only prepared to lose $100 on your trade leaving you with $9,900 at the end of the day should you incur a loss.

The amount of risk that you are willing to take will also depend on the type of trader you are. If you are ambitious and/or experienced, you may find yourself taking a higher risk, say 10%. On the other hand, if you are a new trader or a more cautious trader, then you will probably only risk a maximum of 2%. This amount of risk is also known as per trade exposure or risk per trade.

Make use of order types and analysis

To effectively manage your risk, you will need to make use of your analysis preferences (technical, fundamental, or both) and your preferred style of order types. Generally, a trader would make use of an entry order and a stop-loss order. They may also choose to use the trailing stop. Your trading strategy will help you choose which order types to use.

As you analyze the forex market, you will see what your currency pair is trading at, the trend the market is going for that currency pair. Based on this research and the information you have from your other trading tools, you will be able to decide when you will open a position, how much loss you are willing to take, and so on.

For example, the day has opened. You are wanting to make a trade using GBP/USD. You see that the market rose slightly before going into a dip. This pattern is following yesterday's market pattern. You decide that you are going to spend $100 or 1% of your $10,000 account on the trade. Each pip is worth $2 which gives you 50 pips. You open your position at 1.4053 and set a stop loss order for 1.4003. If the market turns before reaching 1.4003 you may change your stop order to that of 1.4053 so that you make back any losses. You are now implementing a trailing stop.

You continue watching the market and see that you have almost reached the new high of 1.4053 so you allow your order to exit your trade. You reopen a new trade and move the order to exit at 1.4083. The market continues to climb and you close the trade walking away with a 50 pip profit. In this example, you lost and gained in one trade. Fortunately, you managed your losses and capitalized on your profit.

Know when to exit
Know when to exit a trade. If you are incurring loss after loss, stop. Try again later. Often, it's better to exit a trade when you see a string of losses than to continue trading in the hopes of the market improving. Cut your losses and leave until the market is less volatile or has improved.

If you are getting more losses than successful trades, it will be wise to analyze your trading strategy. Although you cannot eliminate losses from your trading, successful trading brings a beautiful balance between losses and profits. You win some; you lose some. A string of losses is an indicator that something is not working in your trading strategy. Stop and reassess. If need be, contact a more experienced trader or financial advisor for help.

Take out the emotion
Emotions are not your ally in forex trading. In fact, they work against you. If you are experiencing a lot of emotional turmoil or crisis in your life, take a step away from forex. Return to trading when your emotions are more stable.

Trading with emotions is a quick way to incur a string of losses. In addition, you need to make sure that the money you use to trade with is your own and not borrowed (except for leverage). Trading on borrowed money adds stress, pressure and anxiety, which are strong emotions. When you trade your own money and have calculated the risk you are prepared to take on each trade, make sure that you are okay with losing that money. If you are not okay with this highly probably loss, don't trade.

If you have doubts about your trading strategy, the amount of risk you want to take, or the market, don't trade. Wait until you are certain about what you want to do. Successful trading is linked to confidence. Do your best to always trade with confidence.
Recommended trades per day

One of the biggest temptations for new forex traders is to go trade crazy. Decide on how many trades you are going to make each day. The more you trade, the more losses you risk. The average recommendation of trades per day is one to two. This keeps you self-disciplined and minimizes your losses. Forex trading is most successful in the quality of your trades, not the quantity. If you make two profitable trades, you have done better than if you made five trades that resulted in losses.

Vary your currency pairs
Another trick in risk management is to vary the currency pairs you buy with. If you buy GBP/USD and buy USD/EUR you are keeping one currency consistent (USD). If the USD drops you will still acquire losses on these currency pairs. Rather purchase GBP/USD for EUR/CHF this way you are able to ride the highs of each currency pair while reducing the losses.

As the saying goes, *don't put all your eggs in one basket*. The key is diversification.

Chapter 6: Trading Psychology

Trading psychology! How do emotions impact your trading success? In this chapter, I am going to look deeply into trading psychology. How do you keep your emotions out of your trading? Is it possible to stay neutral when you are investing large amounts of money?

Keeping your emotions in check will help you to be successful in forex trading. Often, we get caught up in hype or a good run; other times we get anxious as we watch our losses pile up one after the other until all we see is a tower of red loss. In desperation and horror at the extent of our losses, we stop trading. The next morning, we wake up to an improved currency. We pulled out of the trade too early and lost out on the potential profits.

When our emotions come into play, we often can misread the trends or approach trading with clouded judgment. The result? We jump into the trading too early causing a chain reaction of losses before seeing the rise in profits. The key here is timing and perseverance.

With trading psychology, I will help you understand how to keep your emotions from dictating your trading. The hope is to see you succeed and weather the highs and lows commonly associated with trading.

What's happening in your brain?

By nature, people are emotional beings. This is a fact. Most of our decisions and behaviors are driven by emotions. Trading is not exempt from this. Thus, we often are our own worst enemies. We second guess ourselves, questions arise, and before we know it we begin to wonder about conspiracy theories. *Someone is rigging the market!* Our minds spiral out of control.

Our physiology has an impact on our psychology thanks to the chemicals and hormones our brains release throughout the day. Our brains love to release a chemical hormone called dopamine which is motivates us and dictates our behavior. Every time you make a profit or come close to making a profit, your brain sends a rush of dopamine. In essence, dopamine starts to dangle your potential profit in front of you like candy in front of a child. As a result, you become emotionally high on the rush of a win or become set on getting that win.

Our minds begin to rationalize: *one more trade... the market is going to turn any minute now...*

This is the negative effect of dopamine on our psychology and behavior. That being said, our bodies need dopamine in order to function properly. The key is to manage your emotions and exercise self-control.

Signs that your emotions are dominating your trade

One of the best ways to manage your emotions during trading is to know when your emotions are guiding your trading. Some of these signs include being overconfident, greedy, or adamant to turn your losses into profit.

I am going to discuss what I believe to be the five major signs that your trading is being jeopardized by your emotions.

Greed

No matter where we go in life or what we do, greed lurks in the shadows. It watches, ready for the slightest opportunity to whisper in your ear that riches and fame are at your fingertips. Throughout history, we see greed whispering its lies and setting its traps. A prime example are the gold rushes, the colonization of the world in the middle ages, and so on. Today, greed hangs around. This time it has picked trading, casinos, and other investments as its hideout.

When it comes to forex trading, traders fall prey to greed when they do not cash in their profits. Instead, they choose to stay in the trade hoping that they will continue to gain. The danger with this is that the market can quickly turn, resulting in a string of losses. Greed often attempts to seduce traders away from their trading strategy. Overconfidence kicks in and the temptation to keep riding the euphoria of success becomes strong.

Keeping greed under control will go a long way to ensure that your trading is successful.

Fear

Fear has the ability to reduce a trader to a helpless, doubtful, and frozen person. Second guessing comes into play. The trader's trading strategy finds itself flying out the window, abandoned and forgotten.

The trader questions every word that they hear. Research is questioned and their own logic sits down to enjoy a day at the beach while drinking a piña colada.

This debilitating fear creeps in when a trader is unprepared to lose the money they are investing into the market. A fear of loss becomes the cornerstone.

Of course being skeptical and cautious is recommended, especially if you are a new trader. Caution is wise because such a trader will weigh their options carefully, analyze information from charts and trends with a fine tooth comb, and carefully strategize the best logical time to buy or sell. Thus caution and skepticism help a trader move toward success and profit.

Fear, on the other hand, stops the trader dead in their tracks. It also increases the chances of the trader making mistakes and incurring losses or walking away from forex altogether with a string of losses.

Panic
Panic is fear on steroids. When panic sets in a trader will anticipate price dips and market slumps earlier than reality. As a result, they exit the trade too early.
Trader judgment becomes compromised and the trading strategy becomes a distant memory. The second-guessing of how they should trade increases and poor judgment is exercised on the trade.
Finally, the trader walks away with more loss than gain dragging their confidence behind them. A dark day for any trader.

Revenge
Some traders find themselves angry at the string of losses they have encountered. They partner with revenge, launching the "*attack on the forex market*" in the hopes of beating the market and avenging their loss.

The problem with revenge is that it sets traders up for an even greater loss. Revenge clouds the trader's judgment. When they should cut their losses and pull out of the trade, revenge convinces the trader to keep trading. The outcome is exacerbated losses.

Euphoria
A string of successful trades has occurred; the trader is on a high thanks to dopamine. An experienced trader will have more practice at remaining vigilant and skeptical whereas a new trader is easy prey to euphoria.

Euphoria brings with her illusions of grandeur and the belief that every trade will end in profit. She convinces traders that their strategy is flawless, the understanding of trading impeccable, and the market is in their favor.

Thus, the trader doesn't sell when they should. All logic disappears along with the truth that a string of successful wings does not guarantee the next trade will be successful. Euphoria is often the cause of over-confidence.

The danger with euphoria is the increased risk of high losses. The victim trader will soon watch all their profits vanish before their eyes. This opens them up to emotions such as anger, depression and devastation.

The pattern of trading psychology

Generally, traders follow a pattern in their psychological approach to trading. Understanding this pattern or cycle will go a long way in helping you control your emotions while you trade. This in turn will help you stay neutral in your trading and increase the likelihood of you remaining in forex trading as an investment while seeing the fruits of your patience and perseverance.

As the saying goes, *knowledge is power*.

According to Sean Hannan, there are fourteen stages to this emotional pattern. They are as follows:

1. **Optimism** – The future looks bright; investment looks promising, so we buy.
2. **Excitement** – For a new trader, the thrill of a few successful trades is a rush encouraging more trades. The same can be said of a more experienced trader who becomes excited and confident that their strategy, knowledge, and techniques are paying off.
3. **Thrill** – The forex trader is on a high. Confidence is kicking in. What could go wrong?
4. **Euphoria or overconfidence** – A succession of successful trades has occurred. The trader begins to relax on risk management after all what could go wrong?
5. **Anxiety** – The market swings. A series of loses begin to occur but the trader consoles themselves that it will be ok.
6. **Denial** – The market hasn't corrected into appreciation. Value continues to drop. The trader begins to deny any poor decisions. Alternatively, the trader denies that the market could get worse.
7. **Fear or despondency** – The trader has experienced a lot of losses and watches the

market continue its downward trend. Despondency sets in and they begin to think that this is it, the market will not correct and they will not get a profit or at the very least make back the money already lost.
8. **Desperation** – The trader looks for any sliver of hope that they can make up for the losses ensued.
9. **Panic** – Hopelessness sets in. The trader is uncertain of what to do next. They feel overwhelmed, at a loss, and helpless.
10. **Capitulation** – The trader decides to sell. The losses made in the forex trading (which are theoretical until the trader leaves the trade) become real. The trader leaves the trade.
11. **Despondency** – The belief that forex is not a worthwhile investment sets in and the trader decides that participating in forex trading is not wise.
12. **Depression** – Doubt and regret sink in. What did they do wrong? What should they have done? Question after question arises and the trader mulls over the trades further aggravating their depression.
13. **Hope** – The trader may still continue to watch the forex market. Eventually they see the market turn and their chosen currency appreciates in value. Hope stirs. Maybe just maybe forex trading is worth another chance. The realization that the forex market consists of cycles and trends becomes a eureka moment.
14. **Relief** – The trader acts on their hope and begins trading again. A few successful trades occur convincing the trader that forex is still a good investment.

Practical solutions

Given that traders cannot remove their emotions and place them in a jar for later use, managing emotions is important to help you be successful. How do you manage your emotions? What can you do to keep yourself logical, rational, and analytical in your dealings with the forex market?

1. **Understand the forex market and what trading entails** – Do your homework. Make sure that this is an investment you want to pursue.
2. **Have a trading strategy** – Find a strategy that fits your character and method of trading. Become proficient in this strategy. Own it. Your strategy is your best friend, your partner in trading.
3. **Risk management** – No trade is immune from loss. Approach each trade expecting to lose. Be sure that you are absolutely fine with losing the money that you have invested. If you are not okay with losing this money, then do not trade. Implement good risk management strategies (see Chapter 5 for more on risk management).
4. **Be organized** – Track your trades with a trading journal. This will help you pick up trends, patterns, and successful trading methods. You will be able to use this information to fine tune your trading strategy into a well-oiled machine. That being said don't get overconfident. Just because your strategy is being perfected does not make you immune to losses.
5. **Remain skeptical and vigilant** – Keep a level head. Trading is all in the logic and analysis. The more neutral you are the better your trading experience.

6. **Trading is a business transaction** – Know when to call it quits or when to hold on. If you view trading as a business, emotions take a bit more of a backseat so that you can get on with… well… business.
7. **Mistakes are growth opportunities** – Keep your confidence levels high. This will help you to be adventurous and try new tactics or strategies. Yes, you may encounter a few more losses or make mistakes but, you will grow and adapt your trading strategy accordingly.
8. **Losses are part of the trading game** – Losses are not personal to you nor are they a reflection of who you are as a trader. Losses are part of the trading experience. You will win some and lose some. It's not personal. Manage your risks and tweak your trading strategy while sticking to it.

Chapter 7: Do's and Don'ts to Forex Trading

Now that we have looked in some detail at what forex trading is, how it works, its terminology, analysis, risk management and so on, let's have a look at some of the do's and don'ts of forex trading. These do's and don'ts will go a long way in helping you to be successful in forex. After all, why reinvent the wheel when you can take what has already been learned, apply it, and tweak it?

This list of do's and don'ts is not massively long. That being said, these guidelines will help you become a successful trader. Think of them as a checklist.

Do's
1. **Take your time to understand the forex market**. Become intimately aware of economic, political and global trends, events and news. Take the time to understand what is happening in the economic and financial markets. Understand why the collapse of a European country's financial system will affect the EUR at large. For example, when Greece went bankrupt a couple of years ago. Another fantastic example is the collapse of Wall Street before the Great Depression. Understanding the markets, what they are doing, and how they are affected

will help you know when to hedge your trades, when to enter or exit a trade and so on.
2. **Use your trading strategy**. Let your trading strategy be your best friend. It will keep you focused on your goals while breaking them into achievable milestones. One victory at a time is the road to success. Sticking to your strategy will keep you from engaging in impulse decision making, keep your emotions in check and help you take action when the time has come.
3. **Understand the risk to reward ratio.** How much gain to how much loss. Is it worth the risk?
4. **Do your research**. This includes your analysis whether fundamental, technical or both. Read the charts; understand them.
5. **Watch the market carefully** to pinpoint the most optimal time for entering trade.
6. **Be patient**. Trading on the forex market is not about sitting on the computer staring at charts and forex fluctuations. It is taking your understanding of the market and making a calculated guess as to the timing of your entry and exit. If in doubt don't trade. If you rush you will make mistakes and lose.
7. If you are new to forex trading, I highly recommend taking the time to **practice on a demo account**. A demo account gives you a simulated market based on the current markets that you can trade on with simulated money. This will help you learn the forex trade while you develop your forex strategy.

For example, a pilot will often practice on flight simulators as part of their training before flying an actual plane. Often the time spent preparing is worth it in the end. Practice, practice, practice. If all else fails, practice some more.

This is also a great opportunity to test the waters to find out if forex trading is really for you. The best part, is it won't cost you much to practice whereas practicing on live trading could cost you before you see success.

8. **Be aware that currencies move in small frequencies**. This means that even a slight fluctuation can cost you. This is also why a lot of trading in the forex market is with higher amounts of money than other investments. The more money used to trade, the higher the loss is in the grand scheme of things. Forex trading is high risk with high gains.
9. **Be prepared to trade at odd hours**. Since the forex market is open day and night from Monday to Friday, you may find yourself trading early in the morning or late at night.

Don'ts
1. Trade when the **market is inactive**.
2. **Rush**. Plan your trades carefully. Only trade when you understand what the market is doing.
3. **Risk your capital**. Only trade the amount of capital you are prepared to loose.

4. Don't **trade with your emotions** or out of a place of greed, overconfidence, or fear. If you are feeling emotional, take a break and come back when you are more neutral and composed.
5. **Trade when the market is unstable**. Wait for the market to begin correcting itself. This will keep your losses to a minimum while increasing the chances of making a profit. The idea is to enter the trade as the market is turning and ride the wave of currency appreciation.

Chapter 8: Tips and Secrets to Success

The forex world consists of veterans, current traders, and novices, all with the same goal; namely, success in forex trading. Although forex trading has only been online for less than seventy years, the experts and successful have found some common tips and secrets to their success.

As a trader, you can take these tips or secrets and adapt them to your trading experience. At the end of the day, your success is yours to pursue. Everyone's experiences are different, even though the principles remain the same.

In this chapter I am going to give you ten tips to trading success. As you apply these tips, you will find yourself more equipped to pursue a long-term relationship with forex training.

1. **Goal** – Forex trading is no different to any other part of life. It needs goals. Most new forex traders often fall prey to ambitious, gorgeous goals that unfortunately are unrealistic or unachievable. You need to set yourself an overall goal for your forex trading. Once you have identified what your purpose for trading is, you will be able to set up small yet achievable goals. These goals will keep you accountable,

disciplined, tenacious and on track in your forex journey. The road to success has many bumps along the way but your goals will help give you the courage to continue. Your goals will also help you to keep a level head. Emotions are not your friend; goals, logic, analysis, and information are.

2. **Broker** – A broker is another name for an online trading platform or the middleman between you and the buyer of your currency. It is the medium through which you conduct your trades within the forex market.

    When it comes to finding yourself a good online platform or broker, you need to do extensive research. The platform/broker must fit with your trading strategy and plan. Everything about your trading experience needs to be supported over and above your predetermined strategy, goals, style, and personality and so on.

    Compare and contrast a variety of platforms against each other. Do not settle for the first platform you find. You are entering a long-term relationship with your broker so taking your time to make sure that you are happy with your broker and what they have to offer is paramount.

3. **Patience** – When a fisherman goes fishing, he takes his time to get his bait organized, his gear is ready, and his lunch is packed. He is familiar

with the habits of the fish he enjoys catching (perhaps trout or bass). He knows the best time to fish is early in the morning and the weather conditions have to be a certain temperature for his fishing expedition to be successful. A fisherman is patient. He sends his line out into the waters. He waits... and waits... and waits. His line tugs. He reels it in only to find he had not caught a fish. Instead, his hook had snagged some reeds. So the fisherman starts again. He is patient. He waits some more. Some days he is successful, other days he is not. This fisherman fishes because he loves it. He has come to the realization that the process of fishing is more rewarding than the thrill of holding a caught fish in his hands.

Forex requires patience. Patience to understand all the quirks and goings-on of the market. Patience to decipher charts, to know when to enter the market and when to exit. As with fishing forex will reward its traders with a profit. Likewise, it will send your way a few losses. The secret is to not give up which brings me to my next point.

4. **Perseverance** – Don't give up. Keep at it. There is a time to stop trading and a time to hold on. Learn when to do each one – it's part of your strategy. When the losses come, don't allow them to deter you from trading. Keep at it. You will eventually make a profit. Forex trading is an art of its own. It takes practice, patience, and

perseverance to become successful. Giving up never made anyone a success. Seek the advice of trading experts and veterans. Learn as much as you can. Through it all stick to your strategy.
5. **Research** – Yes, you need to understand the forex market, trading, and so on. Most importantly, you need to go on a journey of self-awareness unless you already have a good idea of your character and personality.

   Knowing who you are and what triggers you to positive or negative behaviors and emotions will help you to work out a trading strategy that is tailor-made for you.

   Are you the kind of person who can only trade during the day because your anxiety levels will spike if a trade is left open throughout the night while you sleep? Are you disciplined? Patient? Emotional? Do you enjoy politics, economics, charts, and trends? What is your financial situation? What is your motive behind forex trading?

   Your answers to these questions will help you to avoid a personality mismatch which only raises loss and stress in your life.
6. **Charts** – Whether you adapt technical analysis, fundamental analysis or a mix of both, you need to read your charts. Be aware of what is happening in the forex market at all times. Your analysis techniques need to be adaptable and

flexible, however, your consistency and dedication to understanding your analysis is vital to successful trading. You will be able to make an educated decision on when to exit or enter trades optimally.

When it comes to your charts, you need to analyze both the long-term charts and the short-term charts. The long-term charts will give you the overall movement of the market in the future. It may be headed for a dip. In order to confirm the information you receive from such charts, look at the short-term charts, such as daily, hourly, weekly charts. Before you make any decision these charts need to match. If not, wait.

Remember that the long-term analysis charts tell you where the market is going while the short-term charts show you when to make your entry or exit in the market.

7. **Journaling** – Record every trade you make. Include in your record your emotional states, your approach, and the moment you entered the trade and when you exited the trade. What was happening in the markets? Record the charts of what your analysis was telling you on the day. Make a list of what you did right and what you did wrong.

Journaling will help you stay objective. It is a useful reference for those moments when your emotions begin to dictate your trading. You will be able to pick up on your personal trends which will help you to adjust your trading approach and strategy accordingly. You will be able to keep track of your goal achievements and those moments when you failed. You can also record the lessons you learned and how you grew from them.

8. **Consistency** – Be consistent. Stick to your strategy and goals. Chopping and changing will only result in a string of losses. The best test of your strategy and goals is time. As time goes on, you will find out if your strategy works or needs tweaking. Be consistent with every dynamic of your trading from the analysis to the strategy. Keep at it. Time is your friend, not your enemy. Allow time to communicate with you about your trading. Being consistent amidst losses takes guts.

9. **Managing your money** – What is your view regarding the money that you are going to use in trading? Your view will affect how you react to losses. If you cannot write off the money you trade with in a similar way to a night out, then you should maybe wait until you don't need this money. You need to be ok with losing the money you trade with. This will help you accept the losses that are coming your way in trading. Yes, you will lose. Are you ok with that? Can you

persevere through the losses towards the successes?

10. **Weekend discipline** – When it comes to forex trading, you don't get a weekend or holiday. You need to keep up-to-date on what is happening in the markets, politics, and economics. The weekend is the best time to reflect on the happenings of the week, conduct your analysis, and prepare for the upcoming week. The weekend is your preparation time. The better your preparation, the more likely you are to maintain objectivity, accept loses and hope for success.

Chapter 9: Getting Started

The time has come to put what you have learned into practice. All this information is whirring in your head. Your excitement is married to anxiety. How do you apply all this information? How are you going to make forex work for you? What if….?

Take heart! I'm going to walk you through the first few steps you can take towards getting started on your forex adventure.

1. **Research** – Forex is a world unto itself. A world that deserves time and attention. Learn as much as you can about forex. Find out where you can attend seminars and courses held by credible and expert traders or financial advisors.

    The internet provides information at the click of a button. You can purchase ebooks, watch tutorials and videos, access online trading tools, and more.

    Learn as much as you can about forex. Talk to other traders and forex veterans on forex platforms for advice and guidance. Most of the time, people are willing to help and share their knowledge.

2. **Find a broker and platform** – To start trading or practicing your trading, you are going to need a broker and a platform. Most brokers come with a trading platform. Research the various brokers you are interested in. Compare and

contrast them. The idea is to find a broker with the lowest spread and the best benefits for you as a trader.

When looking for a broker, make sure that the broker you choose is registered with the Futures Commission Merchant (FCM). Your broker should also be regulated by the Commodity Futures Trading Commission (CFTC).
Before registering with a broker, ask for a free trial of their platform. Experiment with the platform and the tools available to ensure that you are happy with what they provide.
Remember that finding a broker is personal to you as a trader. What one trader prefers may not work for another trader.
3. **Register** – Once you have found the best broker for you, register and open an account. This will often involve you paying a deposit or fee to open your account. After all, the broker needs some real currency to give you something to trade with.

4. **Develop a trading strategy** – Research is a part of the forex business. It will equip you to develop a trading strategy. You may find that initially you start with an idea of a strategy but adapt it as you go along. This is a common way to developing a trading strategy.

You need to find what works for you. Play around. Experiment. Find what works. You might find that you prefer technical analysis over a combination of technical and fundamental. You may prefer a trailing stop order over some of the other order types.

Whatever you choose, give it time to show you whether it is successful or not. Time will help you to iron out trends and inconsistencies. Try not to chop and change your strategy too quickly. Time is your friend.

5. **Be familiar with charts** – The charts of your analysis and trends will help you understand what the market is doing within various time frames. This will further help you plan your strategy or tweak it. These charts also help you to know when you are going to enter or exit the trade.

6. **Reward to risk ratio** – Work out your reward to risk ratio. This will help you implement the appropriate orders for your trading strategy.

7. **Practice, practice, practice.** Practice makes perfect. Practice also exposes those aspects of your trading strategy that are either working or failing. This gives you the opportunity to adjust your trading strategy and continue testing it. The goal is to practice until you have had a string of successes and minimal losses. It would be unrealistic to expect no losses. The idea is to have your profits outweighing the amount of losses before trading live.

   While you are practicing, be patient. You may not be trading live, but you are still trading and the principles still apply.
8. **Go live** – After countless hours and days, perhaps even months, the time arrives for you to test the live forex market. Think of it as going for your driver's license. You've put all the effort

in preparing and practicing. In theory, you should be okay. Now the time has come. The proof is in the pudding.

You'll need to open a live forex account with your broker. From there you will be able to trade with live currency, margin, leverage, and so on. Remember to stick to your trading strategy. You've spent the past while practicing, so your strategy should now give you higher odds for success.

Conclusion

Thank you again for downloading this book!
I hope this book was able to help you to understand the fundamentals of forex trading.

The next step is to continue your research. Doing your homework before starting something new will go a long way in helping you to be successful. Since this book is only touching the tip of the forex iceberg, I encourage you to continue learning about forex trading.
Read more on topics such as fundamental analysis, technical analysis, trading strategies, charts, and risk management. The more you read, the more you will understand. I encourage you to attend forex seminars, take credible online forex courses, and speak to veterans in the forex market. Where possible build a network of other traders who are willing to guide you and support you as you learn the ins and outs of the wonderful world of forex.

As you further your personal education in forex trading, research the endless options of trading platforms available on the internet. Compare and contrast the platforms that grab your attention to each other. How are they different? How are they similar? How are they structured? Will they benefit you? What broker is best suited to you?

These questions need to be answered as you uncover more information in relation to your investment portfolio, goals, and character.

Once you have decided that forex trading is the route that you want to go, sign up on a forex trading platform. Experiment with their demo accounts. Ask questions. Learn. Be open to making mistakes. Remember that you will lose some of your money in the hopes to gain profit.

When your confidence has increased, you are ready to experiment with your own money. My final tip to you is this, whatever money you choose to invest in forex trading, make sure that you are okay to write that money off (in case you lose it). This will help you to keep your emotions out of it. You are now ready to trade.

All the best! May your trading bring you both a deeper education and good profitability.

If you have enjoyed this book, please be sure to leave a review and a comment to let us know how we are doing so we can continue to bring you quality ebooks.

Thank you and good luck!

Book 2:

Forex
Strategies for Beginners and Experts: Making Money with Currency Trading

Table of Contents

INTRODUCTION 4

CHAPTER 1: OVERVIEW OF FOREX 6

CHAPTER 2: MORE ON RISK MANAGEMENT 9

CHAPTER 3: TECHNICAL ANALYSIS – FROM BEGINNER TO EXPERT 12

CHAPTER 4: FOREX STRATEGIES – GOING FURTHER 18

CHAPTER 5: PERSONALITY AND TRADING STYLES 23

CONCLUSION 28

Introduction

I want to thank you and commend you for opening the book, "Forex:
Strategies for Beginners and Experts: Making Money with Currency Trading"
Consider a handyman with a toolbox. Within the toolbox are all the tools a handyman needs to complete a job successfully. The toolbox contains common tools such as screwdrivers, a hammer, cutters, pliers, etc. Almost anyone knows how to use these basic tools or finds them easy to learn. The experienced handyman will also find within the toolbox more specific tools to be used for specific tasks such as wrenches, power tools, or multimeters.
Similarly, this book can be seen as a toolbox with both general and more specific tools to help you with your forex trading. I hope to increase your chances of becoming a successful trader regardless of whether you are a beginner or an expert. When it comes to forex trading, information is king.
This book contains a brief overview of forex trading while taking a deeper look at risk management, technical analysis and forex strategies. Although brief, this book is packed with information relevant to both beginner and expert traders.

Within this book I have used examples to help illustrate the topic being discussed. These examples are not based on current currency pair rates or the forex market.

Thanks again for opening this book, I hope you enjoy it!

Chapter 1: Overview of Forex

What is forex?
At some point in our lives, we have heard the term forex at least once. Forex is also known as *foreign exchange.* We use forex when we trade currencies, buy stocks, or exchange one currency for the other.

The forex market also called *Fx market* or *Foreign exchange currency market,* has been open since the 1990s, making it a central point for people and businesses of all sizes to participate in forex trading. As a result, the forex market has become one of the most lucrative financial investments in the world. It sees a turnover of approximately $3 billion per day.

The forex market is open 24/5 with centers located around the world including Hong Kong, Paris, Sydney, New York, and more. As the day ends in the Western hemisphere it begins in the Eastern hemisphere. Traders can enjoy the rush of forex trading at all hours of the day or night.

Forex trading focuses on the trading of foreign currencies, specifically the major currencies such as US dollar (USD), the Euro (EUR), British pound (GBP), Japanese Yen (JYP), Australian Dollar (AUD), Swiss Franc (CHF). These currencies are grouped into currency pairs. Traders trade with currency pairs selling one pair for another; thus, riding the market highs and lows in order to gain a profit.

To help you identify currency pairs, see the below table for easy reference:

Major Forex Pairs	Nicknames
NZD/USD	Kiwi
USD/JPY	Dollar Yen
GBP/USD	Sterling or Cable
EUR/USD	Euro
USD/CAD	Dollar Canada or Loonie
AUD/USD	Aussie Dollar
USD/CHF	Swissy

How to trade forex

Forex trading revolves around currency speculation, which currency is doing better than the other currencies. Traders watch the forex market for trends, highs, and lows. They strategize, analyze, and gather information to make an educated guess on what currency to buy or sell at a specific point in time. The manage their risk and rein in their emotions. Successful forex trading is all about careful logical and composed trading.

Benefits of forex

You may be wondering what are the benefits to trading forex. As with all investment options, forex trading comes with its pros and cons. Let's look at some of the benefits to forex trading:

1. **High liquidity** – The forex market consists of many traders, trading on the market at any hour of the day. This means that when you want to buy or sell currency, you always have someone who wants to either sell or buy your currency pair. You are never stuck with stock that you don't want.
2. **Flexibility** – Traders can trade around the clock on the global forex market. Regardless of whether you are a part-time trader or a full-time

trader, you can set your trading hours to suit you.
3. **Trading on margin** – This is all about leverage. A trader would invest a small amount of money, say $1,000, and receive an amount of $100,000 to trade with. The margin ration is now 1:100. The idea is to trade larger sums of money at a minimum risk. As a forex trader you can invest a smaller amount of money ($200, for example) into trading than stocks because of the margin amounts available.
4. **Free resources** – Most forex trading platforms allow new traders and experts to trade with a demo account. This is great for trying out new strategies or tweaking existing strategies before entering the live forex market. You can also access many websites that provide articles, ebooks, and online courses for free on forex trading. Let's not forget that some of these trading platforms also provide an option to chat live with a consultant or forex trader.
5. **Forex trading tools** – Forex platforms do take advantage of the latest technological advances by providing their users with relatively new platforms, software and other tools to assist traders with their trading.
6. **Take on students** – A professional forex trader finds themselves in a position to become account managers of other traders accounts and assist beginner traders.

These are just some of the benefits to trading forex. As you can see, forex is definitely an intriguing option to grow your investment funds.

Chapter 2: More on Risk Management

Risk management is the foundation of successful forex trading. It goes beyond instinctive thought. It involves strategy, understanding, and calculations. In this chapter, I am going to explain the risk to reward ratio and give you a few risk management strategies that are sure to help you gain profit in your forex trading.

Risk to reward ratio

The forex market is continuously changing. One minute it is going up before suddenly the currency pair you are trading turns negative and drops. What happened? How do you trade with this volatility? This is the nature of the forex market.

Calculating your risk to reward ratio will help you to trade within the volatility of the market and still make a profit. To calculate this ratio, you need to work out how much risk you are prepared to take for the profit you want. You take your net profit (or potential profit) and divide it by the amount you are prepared to risk. The result is your ratio.

For example, you are prepared to risk $30 to make a profit of $100. Thus 30/100 = 3.33:1 this is a profitable ratio.

Risk management strategies

While these strategies may seem more basic than advanced they apply to any trader, beginner or expert. Risk management strategies focus on keeping your risks to a minimum while you wait for your profit.

1. **Know when to close a trade**. Traders make the common mistake of holding onto a trade too long. This often results from a desire to see their profits meet their expectations. The forex

market does not always meet our expectations. It sometimes comes close. As a trader, you need to know when to cut your losses and go.
2. **Ride the trend.** In the world of forex, you often hear the saying *The trend is your friend until it ends.* This means that you need to ride a trend until you see it end. This helps traders to reap the rewards of their hard work.
3. **Watch your emotions**. When you find yourself getting emotional for any reason, be it an emotional situation in your personal life, a desire to make back your losses, or the desire to hold onto your profits, you may want to consider taking a step back to recompose yourself. Trading with emotions is never successful. Most of the time traders who trade with emotion incur more losses than profits.
4. **Limit your leverage**. Yes, as a trader you have access to leverage. This does not mean that you use large amounts of leverage in your trading. The higher the leverage the more risk you have. Scalp trading requires a higher leverage than other trading strategies and you need to be aware of the risk. How much risk are you prepared to take? It only takes a change in the market trends for you to incur a string of losses or a sudden loss before you have no more capital to trade.
5. **Currency correlation**. For traders who are trading frequently or are more advanced, currency correlation is a great risk management strategy. Currency correlation is all about finding those currency pairs that follow the same trends. You are looking for pairs that **do not** have strong correlations with each other.

Think of currency correlation as a see saw, one currency pair goes down making a loss, but the other goes up for profit. Thus your loss is neutralized by the profit with the hopes that the profit exceeds the loss.

Another correlation tip is to look for correlation on times. You want your currency pairs to correlate on the exact time.

6. **Practice.** Practice reading the market. Practice self-discipline. Practice your trading strategies. The more you practice the more you understand and the more experienced you become.
7. **Keep learning.** Research all the time. Keep up to date with economic and political news. Research more into your analysis and trading strategies. Learn more about yourself. Throughout your trading journey, have an attitude of a protégé learning from the master. This attitude of desiring understanding and knowledge will go a long way in helping you become the best possible trader you can be.

Chapter 3: Technical Analysis – From Beginner to Expert

Technical analysis is one form of analysis that traders use to define the strategies they will implement in their trading experience. The purpose of this type of analysis is to evaluate currency movements by observing and analyzing data from previous market trends and behaviors. Technical analysts are always on the lookout for patterns that will help predict price fluctuations and movements within the current state of the market.

What are some of the foundations that technical analysis is built on?

1. **History repeats itself.** Technical analysis stands on the premise that previous trend patterns will repeat themselves.
2. The best way to identify trends is to **analyze price movement** and the **supply or demand** of currencies.
3. **Price movements follow a trend**. Once a trend is established, the relevant currency will follow that trend until it shifts.

Within technical analysis, traders make use of several different techniques including support and resistance, moving averages, Bollinger bands and trends. In this chapter, we will look at the first three which is believed to be the most popular among forex traders. The idea is to expand on technical analysis at a deeper level while adding tools to your trader's toolbars (particularly if you are a beginner trader).

Support and Resistance

Support and resistance is a common yet highly effective tool in your technical analysis. Most forex traders and other types of traders implement this tool in their trading including the traders at Wall Street.

Support acts as a floor to the prices of the currencies you are trading; its job is to slow down prices from dropping beyond a certain point and hopefully turn the trend back up. Resistance on the other hand is a price ceiling often preventing prices from continuing upward.

Support is affected when a large demand of currencies occurs. This prevents the price from dropping further while pushing it into an upward trend. Resistance works in the opposite. When there is a large supply for currencies the price will bottleneck at the resistance level preventing it from breaking through.

Below is an example of what support and resistance will look like on your technical analysis charts:

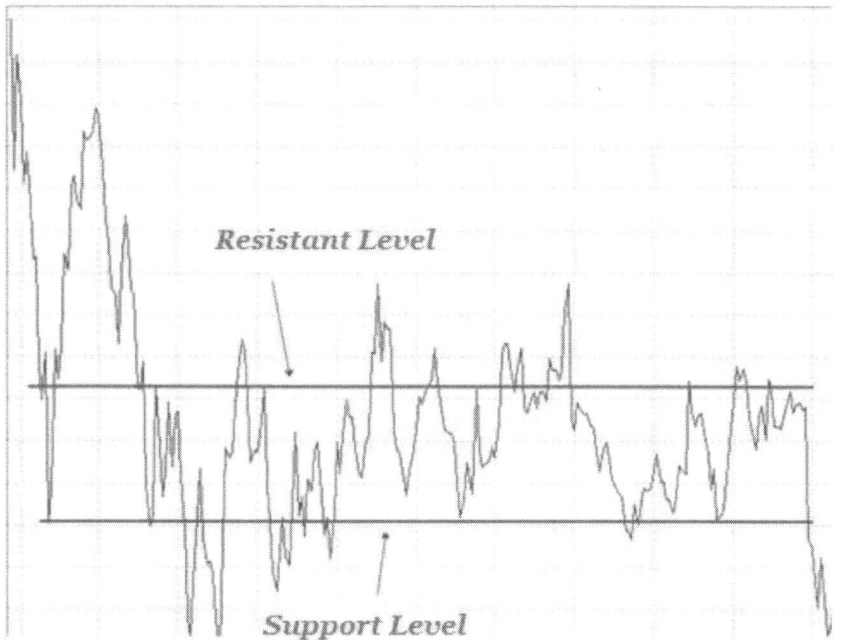

Now that we've established the definitions of support and resistance, let's have a look at three common ways of identifying support and resistance.
1. **Intermediate reversals**. Here you look at your charts for past trends and identify those points where the trends turned (up or down). You then play dot-to-dot by drawing a line across those common points (top and bottom). The line that you draw shows you where the estimated support and resistance lies.
2. **Round numbers**. Psychologically people are drawn to round numbers. When traders see round numbers they will either assume the price has gotten too expensive and sell or they will assume the price is cheap and buy. This in turn changes the current trend in the market and sets a support and resistance level.
3. **Moving averages**. Moving averages are a good indicator of current trends and levels of support and resistance. They show the average actions traders have made with certain currency pairs.

While support and resistance can give you an indicator of when to buy or sell your currencies and where to place your stop loss order, they are not absolute predictions. Always use them as a guide. Use them to confirm your other analysis findings or vice versa.

Moving averages

In lay man's terms, moving averages is the average currency price extended over a certain period of time such as a few days, weeks, or months. The goal of the moving average is to assist traders in identifying trends and when to open a trading position.

The challenge with moving averages lies in their lagging nature. This means that they only confirm a trend once it has already happened. Identifying new trends cannot be done with moving averages whose job is to confirm a trend not establish one.

This leads to an important point regarding moving averages. Moving averages work best with a shorter time frame. In a longer time frame moving averages experience a reduction in sensitivity and accuracy.

Let's have a look at the two types of moving averages:

1. **Simple moving average (SMA).** When implementing SMA, you would specify the time period you want to analyze and you would receive an average for each time frame. SMA gives equal weight to the periods specified. The main problem with SMA is that it is highly susceptible to anomalies. Thus if a currency pair is on an uptrend and a news release is made plunging that currency pair into a negative spiral, your SMA statistics are going to reflect it instead of registering it as an anomaly.
2. **Exponential moving average (EMA).** With an EMA, you will specify your time frames as per usual. The difference comes in the weight on the prices. EMA will provide more weight to current prices while giving lower weight to the prices that started the analysis. Thus if an anomaly occurs it will not throw off your averages.

While you can choose one type of moving average over the other, I do suggest using both at the same time but with different time frames.

One of the most popular ways of reading moving averages is to implement the crossover trading strategy. The price of your currencies will move from one side to the other ending in the close. This helps the trader determine their exit and entry points.

When a crossover crosses below a moving average, the trader knows that a downtrend is occurring and they should close their trade. If a crossover crosses above a moving average, the trader knowns that an uptrend has started. This is a good time to open a trade and cash in those profits.

Bollinger bands

Let's have a quick look at Bollinger bands and how to use them in your forex trading. Bollinger bands were named after John Bollinger. Their objective is to illustrate the volatility of the market. Is the market loud or quiet? Highly volatile or stable? The answer to these questions depend on what is happening in the market.

Bollinger bands are a more illustrative form of support and resistance. Generally speaking, the market norm is between the two bands, namely the middle. *What goes up must come down.*

How do you use Bollinger bands?

1. **Bollinger squeeze.** The Bollinger squeeze helps you identify a breakout. If the bands narrow together at the top, a breakout is about to happen and the price will continue upward. The same can be said if the squeeze happens in the opposite direction.
2. **Bollinger bounce (What I like to call the Bollinger funnel).** When the bands are narrow, the market is quiet, experiencing very little action or movement. When the bands are further apart, the market is considered to be loud with a lot of traders buying and/or selling.

Below is an example of a Bollinger band.

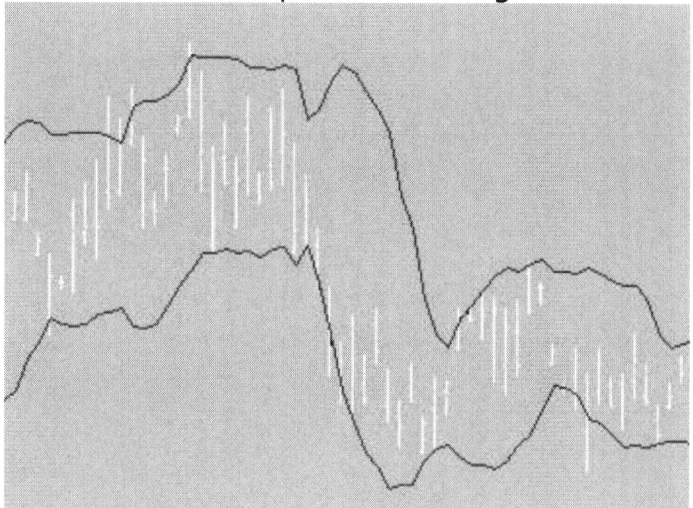

As you can see the white bar charts reflect the price and trade movement of the forex market. The blue lines represent the Bollinger band. In this particular example, the market is quite loud although it quietens down towards the right side of the chart.

Chapter 4: Forex Strategies – Going Further

Forex strategies. Every trader needs them. The more experienced you are in trading the more diverse your strategy portfolio will be. Either way, you need at least one forex strategy. The type of strategies you use will depend largely on your personality. You need to find what works for you. Below are some more advanced forex strategies, however, the bold and daring beginner traders might want to explore them on their demo accounts:

Swing trading

Swing trading typically lasts between a couple of days to a week. Sometimes these trading positions can stay open for a couple weeks although this is not the average. Swing trading is beautifully balanced between the short trading and long trading strategies of forex.

Because of the time lengths, swing trading is a great strategy for those people who are interested in forex as a side income or hobby. These people may not have the time to sit throughout the day studying analysis charts or picking up market trends. Their work, studies, and other priorities are dominant over forex trading. Swing trading is ideal for these traders.

Swing trading requires a couple of hours studying analysis charts to pick up medium trends in the market. The key to swing trading is holding firmly to your analysis. Can you persevere through the dips of the market as you wait for your profit to kick in?

Swing trading focuses on buying currency pairs in the extremes. Ideally, you are looking for those that have been overbought or oversold. As the market returns to a more balanced state, you cash in your profits.

When you are swing trading, you'll be on the lookout for those high volatility and tight spreads. You'll be trading anywhere between 50-200 pips per trade.

A deeper look at scalping

Scalping is another form of day trading. It capitalizes on the slightest fluctuations in the forex market. The difference between scalping and other day trading strategies is found in the amount of time it takes to enter and exit a trade. When a forex trader implements scalping, they will complete a single trade within a maximum of five minutes.

Where most forex strategies allow traders to trade a smaller amount of money, scalping requires large trades to compensate for the small pip fluctuations. In scalping a trade may either lose or profit a couple of pips; the profits are marginable. The larger the investment the more profitable the positive pips become.

A scalper will look to make around 200 trades in a day. This is not an exact amount of trades per day, but my point is that in order to make profits, scalpers need to trade a lot during the course of the day.

This requires intense focus, quick decision making, and dedication. A scalper needs to be able to devote a large amount of time to trading. If you do not have sufficient time available, scalping may not be the best strategy for you.

For scalping to be worthwhile, a scalper's best friend is the stop-loss order. The stop-loss order helps to keep losses to a bare minimum. To be effective, the stop-loss order should be placed close to the amount that the currency pair was purchased. For example, you purchase USD/EUR at 1.2543 your stop loss order might be placed at 1.2544 instead of 1.2548. Thus, you will lose one pip in the event of a loss instead of five pips.

Risk management is key to successful scalp trading.

Positional trading

Most forex trading strategies are day trading strategies; meaning, they do not look at the trends of the market over a lengthy period of time. Where scalping focuses on micro trading and short time frames, positional trading is focused on a lengthy period of time ranging into months.

Positional trading cannot be implemented without a thorough long-term analysis. As a positional trader, you need to be aware of the market trends, history, and other analysis.

Positional trading is the direct opposite to scalping. Positional trading requires a smaller investment than scalping. Usually, traders will not trade more than 2% of their account in a positional trade.

Because you are going to hold the trade for a long time, you will gain a higher pip profit. Traders usually aim to make a minimum of a couple hundred pips in a positional trade. The larger the pips the more profit you make.

Rollovers come into play with positional trading due to the time frame of this style of trading. This is where a loss can easily be incurred. All is not lost. Depending on what your currency pair does, the rollover could either be positive or negative. In the event of a positive rollover, your profit will be rewarding.

Irrespective of loss or profit, you should incorporate rollover into your strategy. Try to cover the cost of the potential rollover in your strategy so that you break even after incurring a loss and negative rollover. This will require a bit of speculation however, it will help manage your risk.

Positional trading hopes to make a profit at the end of a trade or at the very least to have broken even. Ideally, you are wanting your trade to ride out the losses into the profits in order to minimize your risk and losses.

Price action trading

Price action trading is a great strategy for those traders who want a tailor-made strategy and full control. Unlike other strategies that follow specific rules, price action trading is open to each trader's interpretation of the data provided by price action analysis.

How does it work?

If you want the whole truth and nothing but the truth, then price trading is the answer. Because price action trading tells you what has happened it is void of any futuristic predictions. Price action trading is honest. It focuses on marrying technical analysis tools with recent price history in order to identify trends in the forex market.

Price action trading is more adept for short or medium trading than for long-term trading. Although a large amount of trading strategies including price action trading strategies float around the internet, the appeal of price action trading lies in the flexibility to create your own portfolio of strategies. From this portfolio you'll be able to pick out the best strategy for the current trends you will be trading on. This will aid you in improving your profitability while reducing your risk and maintaining a good emotional outlook.

Hedging trading

Hedging is the equivalent of insurance in the world of forex. When a trader implements a hedging strategy they are looking to reduce risk while securing profits. To do this a trader will make use of their analysis whether fundamental, technical or both. The analysis will show the trader where the risk in the market lies, which currency pairs to trade and which currency pair to trade long and short. In hedging, you are looking for a strong correlation between pairs.

For example, you may decide that the best currency pairs to trade are the USD/EUR and the GBP/USD. You look at your analysis and decide to go short on USD/EUR and long on GBP/USD. You've decided that based on your analysis that if the GBP/USD turns over a profit but the USD/EUR renders a loss the difference between the two will still result in an overall profit. At least this is your logical hypothesis. You implement your trading strategy within your hedge. The market moves according to your prediction. The EUR drops and the GBP soars. You walk away with some profit.

In the above example, your hedging worked fantastically.

News trading

News trading borders on the lines of gambling since it is highly volatile and erratic. Some traders love the thrill of watching the market intensely during a significant news release. Intense risk management and zero emotions are needed for traders to be successful in news trading. Traders who implement this strategy have *balls of steel* so to speak.

The challenge with news trading is that no one can predict how the market will react to the news or event. It becomes a *let's wait and see* situation. Only the most daring or most experienced should use this strategy. That being said, if you want to experiment with it please do so on a demo account.

Chapter 5: Personality and Trading Styles

Have you ever noticed how so many of us have these lofty ideas of becoming successful in life within the first couple of years in a new career? Perhaps it's because we all know that we were made for success. This zealous ambition affects all areas of our lives. Forex trading is no different.

Many traders enter the world of forex trading thinking they will hit the *jackpot* so to speak. The reality is that all things in life require dedication, hard work, and patience.

Overall, forex trading should be void of any emotions. This is difficult considering that people are largely emotional beings. Trading psychology is, in itself, a large topic with interesting information. I want to hone it down to self-awareness. If you know who you are and understand yourself, you are better able to manage your risk, choose the best trading style, and know when to walk away for a break.

What is your personality? What trading styles are available?

Know your personality

Forex trading fits two personality extremes: impulsive and conservative. Most people are somewhere in the middle, either leaning toward a predominantly impulsive nature or a more conservative one.

Before we elaborate on these two personality types, let's clarify that there is no perfect strategy to forex trading nor is there a single personality that is ideal for forex. The uniqueness of people is what makes forex trading thrilling and rewarding. You take your unique character and pair it with a couple of trading strategies that fit you. Voila! Success (hopefully). There is no right or wrong personality or trading strategy. The successful strategy is the one that fits you, the trader.

With this in mind, let's explore the impulsive and conservative personality types.

Impulsive

The fickle nature of the forex market plays into the hands of the impulsive trader. This trader can jump into a trade quickly, gain profit, and jump back out. The thrill of the trade, the quick results, and the instant gratification all appeal to the impulsive trader.

However, being impulsive does also mean that as a trader you enter and exit trades too early. The forex market requires traders to judge the entry points and wait for the market to come to that specific level. The problem with impulsive traders is that they often chase the entry levels, eager to get into the market.

Are you an impatient trader?
Can you watch a trading strategy run its course?
How impulsive are you in real life?

Scalping, short-term trading, news trading, and breakout trading are the best strategies for those more impulsive traders. The impulsive trader loves the rush of quick-on-your-feet thinking and reacting. These strategies allow traders the thrill of quick trading as they experience the high of profits and the low of losses.

Conservative

Conservative people by nature are tentative and cautious. They do not want to risk too much, therefore they limit the amount of potential profit they can make in forex trading by not closing trades at the appropriate time.

Their patience is a credit to them. The forex market requires patience. Patience to ride trends and not pull out of trades too early. Patience to wait for change and profit. That being said, forex trading is also about balance. Conservative traders are in danger of being overly cautious thus compromising their profits.

Ask yourself the following questions to help discern if you are a conservative person:

How much risk are you prepared to take?
Are you naturally tentative and cautious?
Are you a patient person or do you prefer quick results?

Conservative traders will generally find that trend trading, hedge trading, and moving averages trading are more suited to their personalities. These strategies allow traders to take their time in a trade, analyze thoroughly, and experience more control over their losses.

Trading styles

Now that we have looked at the two main personality types of forex trading, let's look at how to determine your unique trading style. We will explore time frames and types of analysis. I touched on these areas briefly in the personality types but here I want to expand on them in more detail.

At the end of this section, you should be able to pinpoint a more specific group of forex strategies that you can explore. If you consider yourself an expert at forex trading, you may find yourself rethinking your current strategies and what you can change to improve your continued success in the forex market.

Timeframes

The time frame that suits your personality and trading style will affect the strategy you use and the currency pairs you buy.

If you prefer to trade over a long period of time, allowing the market to develop over the next few days, weeks or months, you will probably choose trend trading. You are riding the trend until it turns.

On the other hand, if you are a trader who enjoys short time frames, you'd probably trade on hourly charts or scalp trading. In this case, you'd make small trades throughout the day. The challenge is finding the currency pair with the smallest spread so that your trades become profitable at the end of the day and not a string of losses.

Analysis

Traders frequently argue over the type of analysis a trader should take. Some advocate for technical analysis while others insist on fundamental. The fact of the matter is that neither is better than the other. What you need to be concerned with is using the analysis that works for you.

When deciding on the type of analysis you use, ask yourself if you prefer using news, economic reports, and other political and financial factors to predict the market. In this case, you might want to implement fundamental analysis

Perhaps you prefer to stare for hours at charts, looking for common behaviors in the currencies. If this is you, you will find technical analysis appealing.

Generally speaking, fundamental analysis is best suited to long-term trading strategies, whereas technical analysis works wonderfully with short-term trading.

The challenge

Although the two personality types discussed above are two extremes, most traders are found somewhere in the spectrum between these extremes.

|―――――――――――――――――――――|
Impulsive   Conservative

The question is, where are you?

For those traders who are aware of their personality style, they may start trading with a strategy that is best suited to them. For a period of time, these traders will probably experience early success. This is great, until confidence turns into overconfidence. Suddenly the traders experiment with strategies outside of their personality style. The result can be disappointing.

This is not to say that experimenting with different styles is discouraged. On the contrary, experiment with various strategies to find those that work for you and the current trends of the market. If you are going to test a new strategy, do so on a demo account until you are confident that the strategy is worth your while and effective. In the meantime, stick to the strategies that you know are working well for you.

Conclusion

Thank you again for reading this book!
I hope this book was able to help you to understand more than just the basics of forex trading. I hope that you received a wealth of information that further equipped you for your trading endeavors. Since forex trading is such a detailed investment, the more information you gain and understand the more you are able to adjust your trading strategy to suit your personality and trading style.
The next step is to continue researching. You can do this by surfing the web, attending seminars and forex courses, or listening to online resources. A lot of resources are available for free on the internet. Talk to other forex traders and your account manager. Ask a lot of questions.
As you research and learn, I encourage you to continue practicing on your demo account until you have a string of profitable successes. This will let you know that your trading strategies are working for you. Once you know this and are confident, you can try on the live forex market. Practice makes perfect.
Through it all, remain flexible and adaptable. Forex is a volatile market, not a static one. You need to be able to adjust with it. You also need to be able to know when to take a step back and regroup.
I also want to encourage you to keep a trading journal in which you can keep a record of your trades, the strategy you used, the emotions you experienced and your thoughts on what personality you have and which trading style suits you. Self-awareness is key to success in any area of life; forex is one of those areas. All the best in your forex trading!

If you have enjoyed this book, please be sure to leave a review and a comment to let us know how we are doing so we can continue to bring you quality ebooks. Thank you and good luck!

Preview of Day Trading

Introduction

I want to thank you and commend you for downloading the book, "Day Trading: The Day Trading Guide for Making Money with Stocks, Options, Forex and More."

This book will introduce you to day trading, starting with the important question, is it right for you? If it is, this book will tell you how to get started, how to make money, how to avoid losing money, and a lot of the technical information you'll need.

Thanks again for downloading this book, I hope you enjoy it!

Is Day Trading Right for You?

> *When J.P. Morgan was asked what the market would do that day, he said, "It will fluctuate."*

"Day trading" means buying and selling stocks so that you close out all trades at the end of the day. When the market closes in the evening, you no longer own any of the stocks you've been trading, and hopefully, you've made some money on your trades. With discipline and knowledge, you can make quite a bit of money day trading – and enjoy doing it, too.

◀ More Random   More Predictable ▶

Gambling — Poker — Day Trading comes in about here — Investing in Stock — Bank Account

You need to understand that day trading is not investment. It is also not gambling. It's speculation, and here's the difference: a roulette wheel at the casino is purely random. Even if you don't know the exact odds on every kind of bet, you can be sure that the casino does. A few people will make a lot of money and most people (except for the ones who own the casino!) will lose money, and it's completely unpredictable which group is which. On the other hand, putting money into a bank savings account is as close to a sure deal as you will ever get in this uncertain world. It's also a rock-solid certainty that you won't make very much money that way.

Investing in the stock market means studying individual companies to determine their real value, and putting money into those that have a good future ahead. If you do this conscientiously, you will almost certainly make money... but there's a bit of randomness in this, and sometimes all the care you can give won't be enough to avoid losing some money.

Playing poker follows this rule: you can't win without both luck and skill, but you can always lose by playing badly. That is, the hand that a poker player draws is determined by pure luck, but what he does with his luck depends on skill.

Day trading has more risk than investing, but also can yield better returns. It depends less on luck than poker, usually pays better, and you don't have to keep that stiff "poker face"! During a single day, a stock's price fluctuates like this:

If this were just a random wavy line, then day trading would be gambling. If you knew exactly where the price of a stock was going, it would be a sure thing (hint: forget it!).

The fluctuations in daily stock prices are almost-but-not-quite random, and it's that little edge of predictability that will allow you to make a profit in day trading. No day trader makes a profit every day, but with knowledge and discipline, you can come out ahead often, better than most people can do by investing and much more controllable than gambling.

What Do You Need to Be a Day Trader?

First and most importantly, you need to be the kind of person who can learn from study, who can make decisions based on rational thinking and not emotions, who can make a plan and follow it, who can lose money without getting upset and make money without getting giddy, and who has at least a couple of hours in the mornings and in the afternoons which can be devoted to day trading with no interruptions.

Next, you need some money you can afford to lose. If you can't afford to lose any money, or you get anxious whenever you do, this activity is not for you.

You need a direct electronic account with a brokerage that offers support for day traders (see the next section).

You should have a fairly new computer with a reliable, fast Internet connection. Here's a tip: if you are using a laptop on your home wi-fi, run a cable from the router directly to your computer's ethernet port and connect that way instead. It will be faster and more secure. Trying to trade on a non-secured wi-fi network is just asking for trouble, so don't try to pursue this career at the coffee shop. It's very handy to add a second monitor if your computer will support this.

Finally, you need time to learn and study before you launch into day trading. Spend enough time doing fictional, practice trades that you can be confident of your decisions before you trade for real.

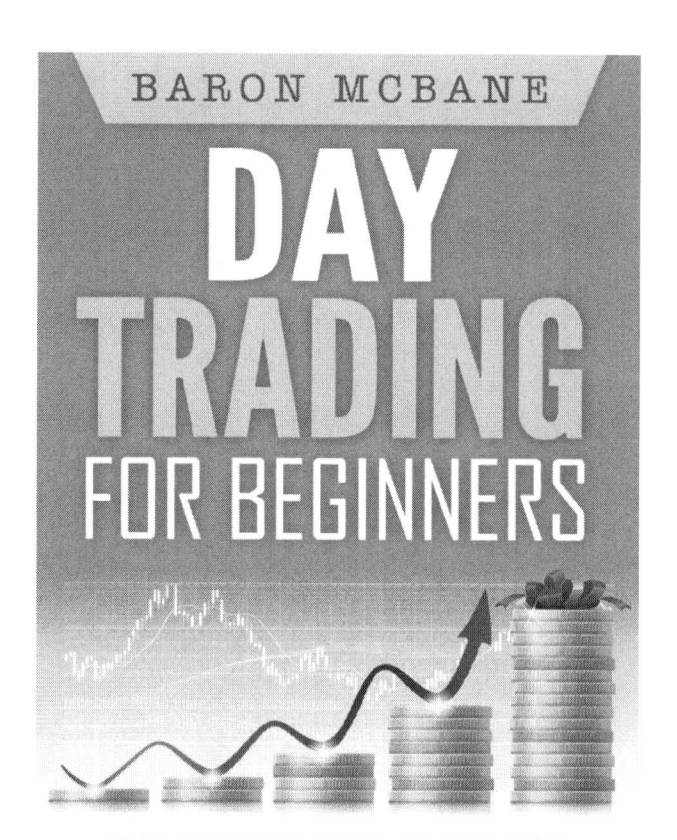

This book is available on amazon.com

Engulfing candle.

green red

bigger then f.M.   vice versa